I wanted to live deep and suck out all the marrow of life . . . and if it proved to be mean, why then to get the whole and genuine meanness of it . . . or if it were sublime, to know it by experience . . .

—Henry David Thoreau

to know by experience
outward bound   north carolina

by

Dan and Diane Meyer

photography by

Dan Madden

Artcraft Press
Morganton, North Carolina

Library of Congress Catalogue Card
    Number 73-83707

Third Edition 1977

for

Rufus M. Dalton

Acknowledgments

We wish to thank the participants of the North Carolina Outward Bound School who are portrayed by phrase or photo in these pages. And for their impressions in the form of original verse; we thank Robert Ortiz (Dawn Mother and Harlem); Charles C. Cole, Jr. (Crew, Spoon Scraping, River, and Spending A Day On Top Of A Mountain); and Maxine Woods (untitled epilogue poem).

foreword

One point about Outward Bound that I find very hard to impress upon others is that there is a large gap between the telling and the actual thing.

Those familiar with the experience of Outward Bound will understand the above lament. For them, this book is intended as a personal remembrance and perhaps to help them narrow the gap.

For those less familiar with Outward Bound, the book is intended to provide an insight into the experience.

The format is the photograph and written impressions of the participants. The reality and impartiality of the camera lens comes closest to that of the experience itself; and the impressions of the participants are the most insightful and eloquent on the subject.

It seems especially fitting that a book about Outward Bound portray the participants — for in the final analysis, it is they who determine the experience.

contents

prologue

The following provides a context for the book's impressionistic approach.

Purpose Outward Bound is directed at discovering one's inner resources and the dignity of one's fellow man. Specifically, the experience seeks to instill self-reliance, physical fitness and compassion as fundamental values recognizing there are few opportunities to formulate such values in an increasingly technological and urbanized society.

Relevance Two factors which have perhaps contributed most to our development as a nation and people were the diversity of our backgrounds and the challenge offered by a beautiful and untamed continent. But today we seem polarized by our differences, and we have tamed the wilderness, only to discover we have made it less habitable and less beautiful in the process.

By bringing people from all walks of life together to share the challenges of elemental settings, Outward Bound seeks to have its participants discover that they possess the necessary internal resources to make it — and do not need to rely on escapes from reality; that despite differences in racial, religious or economic background, human beings are more alike than different and can and must work together; that being helpful and compassionate are part of human nature; and that we are natural beings, closely tied to the earth we live upon and with a responsibility to protect its healthful state.

Assumptions On a philosophical level, the program assumes:

- one reveres life for having experienced it in real and dramatic terms.

- that from such experience one learns to respect self.

- that from respect of self flows compassion for others.

- that compassion for others is best expressed in service to mankind.

On an operational level, the program assumes:

- persons have more resources and are more capable than they think they are.

- a small heterogeneous group has the resources within it to successfully cope with significant physical and mental challenges.

- young, as well as older adults, are capable of critical decision making and responsibility.

- more can be learned by presenting problems than by providing solutions or methods.

- a period of extended solitude contributes to the formulation of personal goals and philosophy of life.

- stress and shared adventure are important catalysts in the self-discovery process.

- that perhaps the most important determinant of a person's future is self-concept.

- that significant, long-lasting learning can be achieved through an intensive, short-term experience.

Method Upon arrival, each participant is assigned to a small crew with whom the three and one-half weeks experience is shared. The activities undertaken may be divided into the following phases:

Instruction — Consisting of the better part of the first week, instructional activities include physical and mental problems which must be resolved by the crew; conditioning exercises such as morning runs and aerial ropes courses, and training in rock climbing, first aid, map and compass, route finding and campcraft. The purpose is to develop physical conditioning, and the necessary skills and teamwork to enable the crew to carry out subsequent activities under progressively less supervision.

Expedition — The second week is devoted to the application of newly acquired knowledge and skills in an extended expedition which generally includes back-packing and camping, river crossings, white water rafting or canoeing and rock-climbing. Though the instructors are along to ensure safety, most of the decisions are determined by the crew itself. The purpose is to refine techniques and build confidence and trust within the individuals and in the crew.

Solo — Consisting of three days and nights alone during the third week, the solo is an abrupt change of pace and routine which affords each individual a chance to reflect and consider the past and future. With only the bare necessities of life, uninterrupted by the civilized world and exposed to an inspirational natural setting, a different perspective on oneself and one's place in the world is often achieved.

Service — Sometime during the third week, the crew is given the opportunity of performing a selfless service. Such service may be assisting with a community improvement project such as repairing a playground or school building, or it may be improving a streambed or trail, cleaning a dump or a campground area, or spending a day with hospital patients, handicapped children, or the elderly. Often crew members serve as instructors and involve their guests in some of the Outward Bound activities they themselves have recently mastered. Sometimes the service project is an unscheduled search and rescue or firefighting operation. But whatever the means, the purpose is to experience the manifold benefits of giving of one's self.

Conclusion — During the fourth week, activities consist of a final expedition, a marathon run and the sharing of impressions. On final expedition the crew is totally responsible for setting goals, resolving difficulties and safely carrying through its plan. The expedition is normally three days long and provides an opportunity to apply knowledge and teamwork. The last course day usually begins with a six to ten mile marathon. Not a race, the marathon is an opportunity for each individual to sense personal achievement and endurance. The remainder of the day and evening is spent in composing impressions from daily journals and sharing insights with crew members.

The short-term nature of Outward Bound has prompted many to ask, "What lasting value can such an experience have?" Its founder, Dr. Kurt Hahn, would respond by quoting a passage from Charles Dickens' Great Expectations:

> That was a memorable day to me, for it made great changes in me. But it's the same with any life. Imagine one selected day struck out of it and think how different its course would have been. Pause, you who read this, and think for a moment of the long chain that would never have bound you but for the formation of the first link of one memorable day.

Herewith, some of those days . . .

who are you?
(instruction)

*I realized today that Outward Bound would be hard. I'm scared—
but I would hate myself if I didn't do it.*

I found myself constantly asking to be reassured.
Eventually I began to ask myself for this assurance.

Mind over matter is relatively simple to say.
Putting it into practice requires something else.

The instructors gave me the knowledge of how to strap myself in and to secure myself. They never gave up or got mad when I took so long, nor did they have to push or pull me — I did everything myself. And I thank them 100% for doing what they did — standing by and thinking the same thought I had in mind. If I wanted to do it badly enough I could find a way.

What now?
Just lean back over the ledge and step off.
But there's nothing there!

Hey, this is nice. Beautiful! Why didn't you tell me?
You wouldn't have believed me, would you?

I hated heights and feared them so much, on the zip line I cried for 50 minutes because I was terrified of the height and falling. That 51st minute I jumped and for a few seconds thought I was in hell, but then I started to laugh and at the end of the 400 foot line I was yelling like the rest of the guys.

I learned that everyone had a lot of strength,
and if we used it to support each other,
it would grow.

It's better to make a positive decision than to do nothing.
If the decision is wrong — it's regrettable, but
action is far better than uncertain hesitation.

"I" was replaced by "we."

All you have to do is reach your hand out and they'll grab it.

For the first time I did not shirk my responsibilities.
I began to feel a part of the crew and it was glorious.

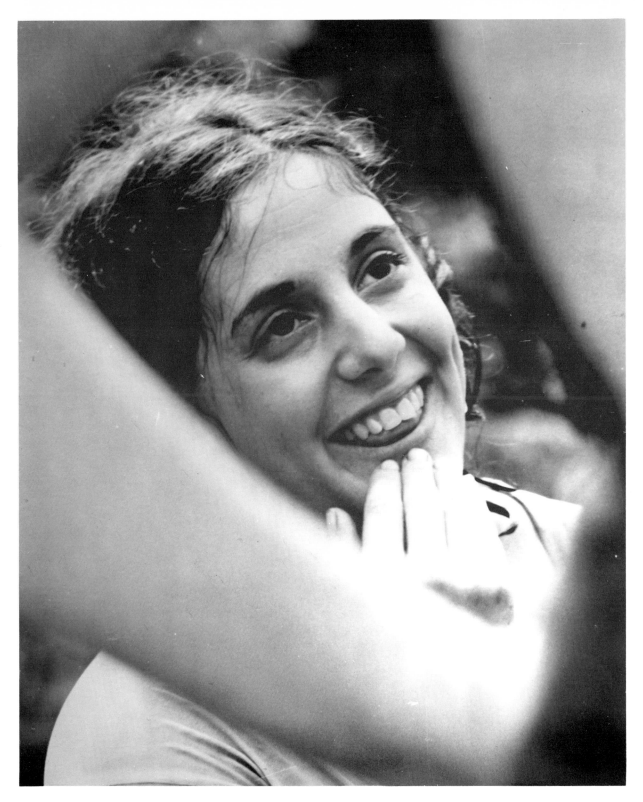

I finally acted on my feelings and not on my feelings about my feelings.

I didn't see why we had to do the things we did, like getting up at 5:30 a.m., and running and dipping. I didn't see any sense in going through the ropes course or standing out in the pouring rain all afternoon. I got sick of it all really fast, so I left. But, once I left, I just couldn't face myself. I guess I was just looking for an easy way out. I've always taken the easy way out of things, and at first Outward Bound was not going to be an exception. After I left, I started thinking about my life and the way it's been, and I really got sick. I guess I felt like about the biggest cop-out alive. So, I came back, and I've found that to be the best decision I've made in my life.

who are we?
(expedition)

CREW

We are so different in our moods,
Our styles, our personalities.
Some like to push while others plod;
Some like to talk, some sing all day
While others keep thoughts to themselves;
Each of us has our separate strengths,
Our limits, fears and untold dreams;
Each of us shows our special skills;
Each learns from what the others know.
We are so different, yet alike;
We are a part of all mankind;
Our striving brings life harmony.

It is wondering what in the world we are here for . . .

. . . and finding the answer in a smile or in a sunny day.

After the bushwack our mood was one of quiet strength and peace. Some walked in silence, others spoke quietly, sharing a part of themselves with companions. When we reached the camp that night, sleep came easily — we had chosen to do more than was required — and had done it well.

For the first time I realized I need others — and I saw people needing me.

Learning I can be dirty and wet — and live
  through it.
Living in the present — neither remembering too
  much of the past nor dreading or fantasizing
  about the future.
Feeling at home outdoors.

I was thinking today that I would miss asking people how their feet or knees or backs were, and miss being asked; that I would miss the feeling of a shared arrival of a long anticipated destination; and that I would miss these very different characters whom I've come to know and care for.

*Below us, the brown river we forded earlier, and around
it the endless maze of green leaves, all seemed to form
one memory of sweating and cursing and trudging through
the cold rain. It was climbing through the briars, thickets, and
rain that had brought people together, so that when the
trail was found and the storm broke, something broke in the
crew. Maybe it was a feeling we had earned our togetherness
and the right to sit on the mountain edge. We found a lot
to see there, a lot to hear in the winds, and a lot that wanted
to be said as the sun set behind the ridge . . .*

DAWN MOTHER

Dawn mother of light, why do you appear in such silence?
Why do you walk in such peace amidst the forest?
Is it that you do not want to awaken the sleepy children of
the wilderness?

Awaken, awaken! It's here! Look how the golden light shines
through the trees. See how the flowers open their hands to
feel its warm breath. I can hear the sounds and cries that
arise from the birds to meet its coming.

*I learned by failure as much as by success,
the need for doing the small, seemingly unimportant jobs.*

This was the first opportunity for many of us
to work and associate in an environment of equality —
not only of rights but also of responsibilities.

SPOON SCRAPING

The scrape of the spoon on the mess kit cup
Is a friendly sound that I hear when I sup.
It goes clink-a-tink, chink-a-link, plunk-a-too
And I know from the clang that the feasting
                    is through.

But the scrape of the spoon is more than a sign
That the food in the cup is now down to the line
For it means that we think it a good tasty stew
When it goes clink-a-tink, chink-a-link,
                    plunk-a-too.

Spoon scrapers who linger long after the meal
Are also expressing the joy that they feel
To be part of this close, loving, confident
                    crew
And we say clink-a-tink, chink-a-link,
                    plunk-a-too.

My lack of confidence and even fear at times stuck out like a sore thumb; but surprisingly, I was not met with derision and ridicule, but the cheers and encouragement of my newly-discovered comrades, students and instructors alike. I began to feel then that indeed I would "make it through."

Now look, if we go too far to the left we're going to get hung up on those rocks. We want to go right down that chute.

I think it would be better to take a chance with the rocks.

Aw, we can do it!

Why don't we walk around this one?

Look! They just made it through. If they can do it, we can do it!

O. K., let's give it a try.

Let's get lined up. A little more to the left. That's good.

Watch that rock!

We're doing fine. Here goes!

Now! Draw! Draw! Draw!

Hold on! Whoooooooa!

We're through? We did it!

That's the best we've done so far! Allllrrright!

RIVER

Soft and beseeching, the river calls.
We turn our sleek canoes downstream;
Ahead we hear the white water falls;
We float through drops of sunshine's gleam.

We see the V's that mark the rocks;
We draw and pry to stay in line;
We reach the chute and plunge ahead,
Ride swiftly on the wave's broad spine.

Glide on the river's vibrant breast,
Merge with the current's constant flow,
Paddle to meet her harshest test,
Feel time's deep pulse as down you go.

*Putting your life in someone else's hands
is an experience that more people should have.*

One crucial point that I appreciated was that I couldn't stay in one place on a rock face for any period of time since my strength waned and I was unable to go further. Life is made of similar substance since stagnation, or lingering foolishly, will ultimately lead to a fall.

*Once you have looked fear in the face and have overcome it,
you can do it again and again and again.*

HASTY RAPPEL.   It was a hard climb to the top of that rock spire where we were to bivouac. On our narrow perch, fixed to a safety line and huddled in our ponchos, it promised to be a long night. All but two were up before the rain clouds moved in and the lightning began to flash in the distance. We could endure the rain, but couldn't chance the lightning. We had to get down, and fast! "Through the carabiner, over your shoulder, and grab it behind your back with your right hand. O.K.? Go!" Down into the darkness, feeling for the rock with our feet. Finally the wet ground. "Off belay, off rappel, all clear, thank you." A shallow cave gave us protection while the skies cleared and the stars came out. We huddled through the night, waiting together to welcome the grey light of dawn.

*(He had been brought back from the expedition early.
His mother had called saying his father would be
entering the hospital and thought her son should
come home.)*

> *"I know it's not an emergency, mom just wants me
> close by. I really don't want to leave, but
> I've decided I'm needed there. You know it's
> funny, I told everyone I was coming here because
> it was my last chance to be a boy — and instead
> it's my first chance to be a man."*

who am I?

(solo)

From the moment that I stepped out on my rock, I was awed by the immensity of my surroundings and my comparative insignificance. I experienced a strange feeling. I had the desire to throw myself into the valley below. Throughout my solo, the urge recurred, and I tried to imagine why. I saw myself sailing out over the valley, arms outstretched, trying to grasp the hills and trees into me. I believe that this feeling was a manifestation of the growing feeling that I am nature and the mountains and trees are a part of me. I wanted to grab them into my arms, bring them into me, and drink in all that they had to offer.

beheld beauty, its secret, its inner soul. The trees, the rocks, the grass felt my naked skin as I felt theirs. I was not man, I was them and they were me. We were one, skin to skin.

Life wasn't governed by the clock and my mind and bodily self rejoiced at sensing the more steady and reassuring pulse of nature.

I became intensely aware of the bond between every particle of creation and myself. I saw beauty I had never known. I sat and looked at the falls and I learned something about love. As I see something of myself in another, I begin to understand him. This understanding seals a bond between us. In the same way, does it not follow that because I recognize something of myself in a waterfall, a bond is created between the waterfall and me? Else why should the sight of the waterfall make me so happy?

SPENDING A DAY ON TOP OF A MOUNTAIN

What have I done today upon this ledge?
Produced no goods nor made new capital,
Constructed no new building for the state
Nor planted, ploughed or harvested food;
I did not buy or sell a single thing
Or add a cent to spur the nation's wealth.

But here immobile on this mountaintop
Neither did I destroy another's hoard,
Consumed no fuel, took no resources from
The ravaged earth, bartered away no land,
Injured no stranger, spurned no seeking friend
Nor joined the world's mad clamoring for more.

What I have done is better weighed in years.
I watched the morning mist rise on the wind
And heard the hunting hawk sing spiraling;
I smelled sweet laurel, watched the lichen grow,
Counted pine cones, caressed tree bark and rock,
And saw the sun's clouds shining as it set.

I feel that I've become a part of the land and the land a part of me.

I found myself making many analogies on my solo. All the trees around me were blowing in the wind — while those far away didn't show any life. It seemed like people. If you look close enough, all have the same feelings — though it's so easy to ignore if you only look on from afar.

It let me see and feel how man was meant to live.

I came up with a few thoughts I'd like to share with others: Standing by a controversial belief is like holding onto a sizzling rope; if you let go you can't regrasp it; however, if you hold on, you must be willing to bear the pain;

Uphill climbing is best for the mind as well as the body, for the mind is searching for a higher tomorrow and the body is groping for the next foothold.

I made a better friend of myself.

I thought a lot and wrote, and a few times I cried because I was lonely. My greatest achievement was to make it through each night since I have always been afraid of the dark. I was not afraid at all for some reason.

I never felt alone. Was it because I was always surrounded by life? Or because the sun became my playmate? Or was it really because there are people far away who love me and I can sense their company?

I was very satisfied on my solo, as I enjoyed being "with myself"— which is quite different from feeling just "by myself". I felt if everyone had a chance to live alone, then they'd be able to live together better.

who we are!
(service)

You really had to be involved; that was the thing. If someone got hurt, no ambulance came and you couldn't just ignore — you had to help no matter how panicky you felt.

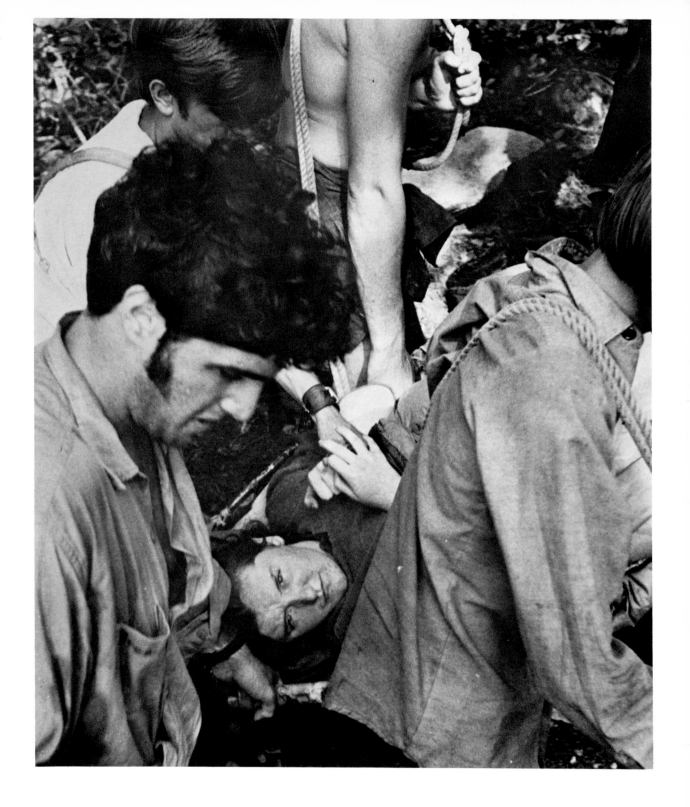

I remember flipping into the falls with my raftmates
and the unequalled feeling I had when I saw that everyone was safe.
We laughed and cried and embraced and felt life to the Nth degree.

Though I may not have any deeply profound things to say, that's
probably what I liked best about it — it was there; it was real.
We did it and maybe someday the full consequence will circle around
and give each of us, wherever we are, a little
encouraging shove from behind.

Here I lived in a large family for the first time in my life.
Everyone really touched and influenced me in some way,
be it little or grand, whether they realized it or not.

We were not always on time, but we were late together.

epilogue
(who I am!)

I made the marathon. I didn't think I would.

I've done things which I would never have trusted myself to do — and in the process acquired a new appetite and set new boundaries for what I can do and hope to do.

I can't say that this place has profoundly changed my life — like
say from a pile of bricks to a complete home, but it has provided
the mortar and someone to start putting that pile of bricks together.

For me, it was like taking off a glove
        and feeling the world of real experiences for the first time.
Without the insulation one learns a great deal more about the world
        he is feeling and a great deal more about one's hand.
We all wear gloves, but mine will never be so thick as before.

It doesn't make you a man. It makes you realize you are a man.

I thought that it would and was meant to change me greatly.
It has only shown me my problems and challenged me to work
them out. I have learned that this school, and life itself,
give nothing except an opportunity to learn. This is neither
what I expected or wanted, but what I now realize I needed.

On a solely individual basis I learned that I have a well-spring of
personal resources that remain to be tapped. However, as an individual
functioning within a group, I learned that I have an awful lot to learn.

I was glad to see that I was taken to be made out of bones and blood,
and not smoke and wine.

I have learned that the hardest thing to do when you have a goal is to start, and the next hardest is to continue to push yourself when the going gets rough.

Self-satisfaction doesn't come from accomplishments. It comes from one's own admittance of self-worth.

I didn't discover any universal truths, but I did find out about my own preferences and abilities — and usually I was pleased with what I found.

I realized all I had taken for granted, and how lucky I am. I became neither an astute environmentalist nor a lover of civilization. I came to appreciate the need for both, and, at times, the neglect of either.

I learned that you don't need color televisions, fancy clothes or fantastic looks to feel good about yourself.

It's given me a yardstick for determining my productivity. I can never again be satisfied with just getting by.

Mostly I think I did good.

HARLEM

Harlem, if you were to know the joys and sorrows I have felt within this vast and beautiful country, you would welcome me back with open arms. But I know that you are selfish, that your heart is cold to the cries of your children.

So, beware Harlem, with your structures of dirt. I'm coming back to conquer, for I have seen fear and we have become one. And I have felt sorrow and pain and joy at the hands of the greatest of all powers — nature.

Harlem, you are nothing but man's inhumanity to man and I will be the victor for determination and will are on my side and I will not be overcome for I am real and alive and you are dead.

The last night of the program, on the way back to base camp, the final stanzas of a poem wrote themselves in my head in a matter of minutes. It was a poem I had been trying to work out for two years — one that encapsulates my personal perspective. I knew then that beyond the aches and pains and the sense of physical defeat of my very tired body, the experience was well worth the trip. When I finished that poem I knew everything was going to be all right.

Everything goes down to dust,
And knowing that I also must,
Why should I live in fear?

No man's word forever stands
Though carved in stone by artful hands.
Each age renews its truths.

For worldly pleasures body yearns,
So to the earth the flesh returns,
The dust reclaims its own.

But soul another journey makes,
Another realm for home it takes,
The One reclaims Itself.

As evening darkens down to night,
Awake within to find the Light,
The Silence there is Shining.

appendix

a history

OUTWARD BOUND began in 1941 at Aberdovey, Wales as a means of preparing young merchant seamen for the demands of hazardous service. The program was based on the principles conceived by Dr. Kurt Hahn, Headmaster of the famed Gordonstoun and Salem Schools. Its success led to the establishment of additional schools serving increasingly broader populations and needs until today there are 35 Outward Bound schools operating on five continents — Europe, Africa, Asia, Australia and North America. The first American school was opened in 1962.

PRINCETON PORTRAITS: JOSH MINER — '43. IS OUR YOUTH GOING SOFT?
PRINCETON ALUMNI WEEKLY, APRIL 28, 1964.

The idea of an Outward Bound school in North Carolina began in the spring of 1964 when Watts Hill, Jr. read an article in the Princeton University Alumni weekly. A true renaissance man, Mr. Hill was president of the Home Security Life Insurance Company, had served two terms in the North Carolina General Assembly, was past director of the North Carolina Symphony and the Art Museum, and had served on a number of educational study commissions, including the National Advisory Commission on Community Relations. After reading the article, he forwarded it to The North Carolina Fund, a private foundation conducting experimental anti-poverty programs, with a note suggesting they might be interested. The note reached Jack Mansfield, the Fund's director of special projects, who began researching the program and eventually assigned his assistant, Marjorie B. Calloway, to work on the project in the spring of 1965.

A Phi Beta Kappa graduate of the University of North Carolina, Marjorie had taught elementary school in Raleigh and in London, England before joining the Fund. Her first duties with regard to an Outward Bound School were to help recruit a Board of Directors. By July, five members had been chosen, including Watts Hill who was serving as Chairman Pro-tem. During that month Mrs. Calloway began a firsthand acquaintanceship with several Outward Bound schools by attending the first Women's Course at Minnesota. In August, Josh Miner, president of OUTWARD BOUND, Inc., traveled to North Carolina to confer with the planners of the school.

N. C. SITE OF A TOUGH PHYSICAL TRAINING SCHOOL?
THE NEWS AND OBSERVER, RALEIGH, AUGUST 8, 1965.

At first the school was planned as a sea school with possible location in North Carolina's Outer Bank region. But a sea school curriculum demanded considerable investment in land and capital equipment, so attention turned to the mountains. In October of 1965. Mansfield and Calloway, together with two Colorado Outward Bound instructors, Herb Kincey and Dave Mashburn, inspected the Linville Gorge area for a possible school site. In December, after reviewing slides and reports on potential mountain and coastal sites, the Board voted unanimously on the Linville Gorge area and authorized Mrs. Calloway to begin negotiations to lease the property. This, as it turned out, was no easy task. Property boundaries which were mutually agreeable to the U. S. Forest Service and the school had to be worked out, as did the protests of many area residents and groups for whom the Gorge was a traditional hunting and fishing ground which they felt would be threatened with over-use.

SELF-CONFIDENCE GOAL OF SCHOOL FOR YOUTHS
DURHAM MORNING HERALD, JANUARY 19, 1966.

In January 1966, the national Outward Bound office approved the school's organization and program, and articles of incorporation as a private, non-profit educational institution were filed in Durham. During that month Mansfield, Calloway and Dr. Richard W. Borden hiked the Linville Gorge area on a publicity and exploratory expedition. Dr. Borden, a pediatrician, was the first appointed Board Member. A decorated veteran of the Normandy and Okinawa invasions, he was and is an ardent worker for scouting and Outward Bound.

On April 13, the school received its charter from the national office and Mr. Anthony Mulvihill was hired as the school's director of development. Mr. Mulvihill, a graduate of Georgetown University, had served as a Marine infantry officer and youth work specialist for Harlem Youth Action and Outward Bound. He and Mrs. Calloway shared the work and the office at The North Carolina Fund until June when Mrs. Calloway became an employee of the Outward Bound School, and offices were established in the Home Security Life Insurance Building, Durham. The long hours, personal dedication and sacrifice on the part of Hill, Calloway and Mulvihill provided the foundation upon which the school was to be built.

The Board of Directors commissioned Mr. Vincent Lee, an architectural graduate student at Princeton, and former Outward Bound instructor, to design the school. The resulting bold yet rustic plans earned Mr. Lee an advanced degree and is an outstanding blend of architectural beauty and Outward Bound purpose. Although never executed, his concept was so exciting it served to encourage the Board at a time when there was little evidence that the school would be established. Mr. Lee supervised the construction of the main building which is still in use, and the general layout of the present school facilities.

PREYER IS NAMED TO CHAIRMANSHIP
BURLINGTON TIMES NEWS, AUGUST 16, 1966.

In August, Richardson L. Preyer of Greensboro was elected Chairman of the Board of Directors. A former Federal Judge and Senior Vice President of North Carolina National Bank, Mr. Preyer had also found time to serve on the Board of Directors of the Y.M.C.A., as Council Member for the Boy Scouts of America, State Chairman of the National Conference of Christians and Jews, and a host of other community activities. The school's scheduled opening was less than a year away and among the things which remained to be done were recruitment and selection of a school director and staff, construction of the school and the recruitment of students. To raise the necessary capital and scholarship funds which would enable it all to happen, Chairman Preyer appointed Griswold Smith of Greensboro as Fund Drive Chairman.

GIFTS PASS $25,000
GREENSBORO RECORD, SEPTEMBER 10, 1966.

On a fall evening, in a driving rain, Lance Lee, a former instructor at Hurricane Island Outward Bound School — no relation to Vincent Lee, arrived at the school site with four young men to build the school. They had stopped on their way from Durham and picked up tools, lanterns, cooking equipment and food. They began their work without the benefit of electricity, plumbing, beds, or decent shelter and with the further limitations of adverse weather and a rock-bottom budget. The "woods crew" remained until mid-December and returned in March of 1967, expanded in numbers, to complete the job in time for the school's opening.

LOCAL BOYS HELPING CLEAR SITE FOR OUTWARD BOUND SCHOOL
GOLDSBORO NEWS, MARCH 27, 1967.

Things now began progressing rapidly and simultaneously. On the site, a main building was constructed from the huge timbers of the former Morganton Furniture Company, donated by Mr. H. K. Phillips; and after some tense moments occasioned by four dry holes, a well was successfully drilled; mobile homes were moved in for temporary housing of staff families; tent platforms were erected for staff and student use; and approximately one mile of road was constructed. Meanwhile, the Board had decided to establish the North Carolina School as the first year-round Outward Bound School in the United States, and backed its decision with over $100,000 in personal pledges. Key support came from Board Member, Lawrence M. Cohen, president of Jewel Box Stores, whose enthusiasm and timely contributions kept the fledging organization operational. The Jewel Box Stores also pioneered in the application of Outward Bound to management training and made substantial contributions to the school's scholarship funds.

ASHEVILLE EDUCATOR NAMED DIRECTOR OF NEW N. C. OUTWARD BOUND
THE SOUTHERN PINES PILOT, APRIL 2, 1967.

James G. Hollandsworth was appointed as the first school director. Mr. Hollandsworth had been a teacher of mountaineering for over three decades and was Dean of Students and Chairman of the Science Department of the Asheville School. The Durham office began recruitment and selection of staff and students for the first course. The instructional staff, drawn from several nations, arrived at the school during May and June. Among them were Knut Smith, John Lawrence, Peter Sheehan, Jack Shirey, Dick W. Day, Lance Lee, Dick Eriksson, and Peter Coburn. George Greene, a retired Marine Sergeant-Major directed the logistical and office operations — a position in which he served for more than 3 years.

On July 2, 1967 the school was dedicated by Mrs. Emma Clark, U. S. Postmistress at Jonas Ridge, and thereupon began its first class of 47 high school and college age men from a wide variety of backgrounds.

THIRD CLASS ENDURES GRUELING TRAINING
ASHEVILLE CITIZEN TIMES, OCTOBER 2, 1967.

For the most part, the program was conducted in the vicinity of the school and focused on cross-country expeditions, rock climbing and mountain search and rescue activities. By the year's end a total of 184 had been enrolled including 25 forestry students from Wayne Technical Institute at Goldsboro who followed the experience with two months' field work for the Forest Service and were granted academic credit for the three-month period.

RUGGED MOUNTAIN SCHOOL GETS NEW BOARD CHAIRMAN — DALTON
CHARLOTTE OBSERVER, SEPTEMBER 18, 1968.

1968 brought a number of major changes in staffing and organization. Following Mr. Preyer's election to Congress, Board Member Rufus Dalton, a business and civic leader in Mooresville and Charlotte, was elected Chairman of the Board and remains so today. Some measure of the esteem in which he is held by those associated with the school is reflected in this book's dedication. Chairman Dalton appointed Roddey Dowd of Charlotte to head fund raising efforts. Mr. Murray Durst, a seasoned administrator with broad experience in training and youth programs was appointed school director.

In order to improve communications and streamline operations, the development office at Durham was closed and functions transferred to the school on Table Rock Mountain.

On the school site, improvements continued with a real commitment to environmental protection and included construction of seven miles of underground power and telephone lines and a waste-water sewage treatment plant.

By the year's end a total of 228 students had been enrolled including 19 in a special course for business managers.

OUTWARD BOUND SCHOOL ENROLLMENT IS DOUBLED
ASHEVILLE CITIZEN TIMES, MAY 1, 1969.

In 1969 significant strides were made in creating a stable base of operations. The turning point was Director Durst's decision to concentrate on a strong summer effort. As a result, enrollment that year doubled to a total of 414. Special courses included one for 83 Upward Bound students, as well as one for managers.

Site improvements necessitated by the expansion included an equipment storage building, shower houses, additional tent platforms, service roads and a second well.

The program that year was characterized by experimentation toward the use of the Great Smoky Mountains, and integration of rock climbing and rafting into expeditions. A beginning was made toward objective program evaluation as Dr. Lloyd Borstelmann, Member of the Board and a psychologist on the Duke faculty, undertook a research study to measure the effects of the experience. Dr. Borstelmann has served all of the staff as counselor and friend, his warmth and concern contributing greatly to the development of the school.

U.N.C.C. EXPLORES OUTWARD BOUND
CHARLOTTE OBSERVER, NOVEMBER 3, 1970.

In January 1970, Associate School Director, Jed Williamson, became Acting Director following Murray Durst's appointment to National Executive Director of Outward Bound. Williamson held a graduate degree in counseling and had been an instructor at the Colorado and Hurricane Island Schools. An experienced mountaineer and skier, he had led a McKinley expedition and served on the Olympic Biathlon team. Under Williamson's direction, the school enrolled a total of 506, in a year marked by special programs including a credit course conducted for East Carolina University, and courses for the University of North Carolina at Charlotte, the North Carolina School for the Deaf, the Webb School and a number of 3-day educators' seminars.

YOUNG WOMEN WILLING AND ABLE AS MEN
MORGANTON NEWS HERALD, AUGUST 17, 1971.

In January 1971, Dan Meyer, with a background in forestry and youth work, was appointed Director. The school's growth continued with an enrollment of 589. Program development included the introduction of women's and college accredited teacher practicia courses, experimentation with semi-mobile and mobile courses, and the refinement of the managers' and educators' seminar courses. Special courses were conducted for St. Albans and Cardozo Schools in Washington, D. C.; Wild Lake School, Maryland; Inroads, a Chicago manpower development program; Earlham College faculty and Toledo public school teachers.

UNUSUAL SCHOOL IN N. C. INSPIRES UNUSUAL THOUGHTS
CHARLOTTE OBSERVER, JANUARY 17, 1972.

Realizing that maximum enrollment levels for the facilities and environment had been achieved, the school sought to stabilize operations in 1972 and enrolled 530. Courses were made more mobile and greater use was made of the Pisgah District lands south of Asheville, and the Great Smoky Mountains. Such dispersment was necessitated by the growing use of the areas by the general public and other educational institutions whose interest in many cases was kindled by the North Carolina Outward Bound School.

Standard courses were offered for men, women, coed and older adult groups. Whitewater rafting was made part of the standard course curriculum. Caving and "urban experiences" (survival and/or service in the city) were offered as optional activities to some crews. Service projects became more directed at human development such as working with hospital patients, foster children, prisoners, etc.

CREDIT OFFERED FOR OUTWARD BOUND
THE APPALACHIAN, MARCH 24, 1972.

Appalachian State University granted six quarter hours of academic credit upon completion of the standard course, thus enabling North Carolina to be the first Outward Bound School to gain such recognition. Involvement with higher education continued with the school's first winter course, which was directed at interim-term college students. And student teachers from Appalachian State University were enrolled in Outward Bound as part of their practice teaching term in a study to explore its effectiveness as a means of teacher preparation.

SELBSTERKENNTNIS DURCH OUTWARD-BOUND-TRAINING
MANAGER MAGAZIN, AUGUST 1972.

岩を登り,激流を下る地獄のしごき NIKKEI BUSINESS, AUGUST 1972.

Other special courses were conducted for Duke University; West Chester State College, Pennsylvania; and Canton Country Day School, Ohio. Managers' courses were conducted in the spring and fall and captured international attention.

That year, Maurice Hill of Morganton volunteered to undertake the school's fund raising efforts which were to be directed at broadening the base of support. As one result, the school became a state approved project of the North Carolina Jaycees who help in identifying students and sources of scholarship assistance.

OUTWARD BOUND SCHOOL: EDUCATION BY DOING
GREENSBORO DAILY NEWS, APRIL 1, 1973

In 1973, a total of 540 students were enrolled, fully one-third of whom were women. Courses for older adults (25 years to 60) were also expanded and accounted for one-fifth of the total students served. Program highlights included: introducing canoeing into the Standard curriculum, using caves and swampslands as optional expedition areas, conducting American Outward Bound's first Juniors Course for 14 to 16 year olds and first Alumni Course, which featured parachuting.

Other special courses included programs for West Chester State College, North Carolina State University (which joined ASU in granting college credit to program completers), and Woodberry Forest School.

Site improvements included the construction of rustic cabins which replaced tent platforms permitting year-round overnight use by crews which now spent the great majority of their time on the trail.

OUTWARD BOUND FUND DRIVE UNDERWAY:
MORGANTON NEWS HERALD, MAY 28, 1973

Former Governor Terry Sanford, who had headed The North Carolina Fund which helped to establish the School, accepted the Chairmanship of the year's Fund Drive to retire the School's capital indebtedness. The drive was concluded at a dinner hosted by Governor and Mrs. James Holshouser at the Governor's Mansion. If ever there was a dramatic example of the School's broad ranging appeal — it is to be found in this effort. By the year's end, $155,000 had been raised — enough to retire the large note which had heretofore been secured only by the signatures (and faith) of those early Board Members.

EVERGLADES TESTS BODY AND SPIRIT

MIAMI HERALD, JANUARY 30, 1974

The School met a sharply increased demand in 1974 by expanding its enrollment to a total of 734. To achieve this level without over-crowding either School facilities or adjacent expedition areas, three base camps were employed: Tablerock, Pisgah and Nantahala, with the latter two being mobile support bases for expeditioning crews. Participation of women approached 40% as most of the course offerings were co-educational in response to the demand. Participation by older adults continued at about 20%.

Program highlights included: a winter course in the Florida Everglades; staff training to goals and procedures prescribed in the School's published Instructor Handbook; the development of highly nutritious, fresh-food trail menus and recipes; and special backpacks which were designed and manufactured at the School. Special courses were conducted for Maryland Parks and Recreation (Howard County), State University of New York (Cluster Colleges), West Chester State College, Pennsylvania, and Brentwood Academy, Tennessee. Consultant services were contracted with Lycoming College, Pennsylvania, Youth Development Bureau, Montana, and Duke University. Davidson College joined the growing list of Schools offering academic credit for the experience.

In order to provide for future growth and an ecologically desirable distribution of crews, the School entered a lease agreement providing joint use, with the Scout troops of far Western North Carolina, of a 100-acre tract adjoining the Nantahala National Forest, near Franklin, N. C.

ONWARD AND UPWARD WITH OUTWARD BOUND

NEW YORK TIMES, OCTOBER 12, 1975

During 1975, a total of 753 were enrolled. Standard winter courses were conducted simultaneously in the Everglades and in the Great Smoky Mountains. Standard summer courses were conducted from Tablerock base, and Green Cove, the newly constructed base camp at Franklin, North Carolina. The Green Cove facility, built primarily by volunteer and permanent School staff, included rustic warehouse — office building, bathhouse, pumphouse, tent platforms and ropes courses.

Special courses included seminars for educators and minority leaders as well as five adult/executive courses. Contract courses were conducted for the North Carolina Child Care Association and West Chester State College.

Service projects focused on outings with mental patients, orphans and retarded children; building a playground for a head-start center; and improving parks in four mountain communities. Two controlled research studies demonstrating the effectiveness of the training were published.

LEARNING HOW TO TAKE IT

TIME-LIFE BOOKS, HUMAN BEHAVIOR SERIES: STRESS 1976

In 1976, an enrollment of 856 indicated that the School was the third largest in the United States. The average age of participants in Standard Courses had continually increased over the years from 17 to 22.5 years. Moreover, significant numbers of middle-aged adults were enrolling in the short courses.

Program improvements included goal-oriented, "linear" expeditions wherein crews backpacked to major activities in order to reduce truck travel to absolute minimum. In addition, greater emphasis was given to nutrition and to cultural history.

Short courses were tailored to middle-aged and older adults from a wide social spectrum. Contract courses were conducted for Joy Manufacturing Co., Southeastern Community College, and West Chester State College.

Community service projects continued to concentrate on the handicapped, environmental protection, and training of rescue workers.

Two special events during the year were particularly noteworthy. In March, a tenth Anniversary Dinner was held in Durham to celebrate this milestone. More than eighty former board members and staff attended including those whose names illuminate this brief history. And as that special evening evoked an idealistic past — the second event signaled a flourishing future. In October, 1976 South Carolina's Governor James B. Edwards hosted a dinner in support of closer ties between the School and its neighboring state in the years ahead.

ADVENTURE EDUCATION — ONE ANTIDOTE FOR FUTURE SHOCK

TREND MAGAZINE 1976

Thus, at the end of its first decade, more than 5,000 men and women from virtually every background have hiked up the School trail to face the challenge of sheer rock faces, whitewater rapids, exhausting expeditions and three days of solitude. Nearly all have met the challenge and thereby gained a greater appreciation of themselves and their fellowman. Fully one-third have received financial assistance from the School to enable their participation. And many have been educators who have initiated similar programs in their own institutions, thereby vastly multiplying the number being touched by this experience.

And it all began with little more than an idea — an idea to which persons of vision and goodwill committed themselves. Nonetheless the successes of the North Carolina Outward Bound School were hard won, and its history is a testimony to its credo, "To serve, to strive and not to yield."